VIOLETS BY DYING STARLIGHT

THE MUSINGS OF A FRACTURED YOUTH

J. M. Catherine

BookLeaf
Publishing

India | USA | UK

Violets by Dying Starlight
The musings of a fractured youth

Presentation by BookLeaf Publishing

Web: www.bookleafpub.com

E-mail: info@bookleafpub.com

ISBN: 9789358360295
First edition 2021

ACKNOWLEDGMENTS

Firstly, I would like to thank everyone in the team at BookLeaf Publishing for making this book happen. If it were not for your tireless work and dedication this piece would still be a word document on my computer.

I would like to thank my mother, Narda, for being the one who passed down her gift for writing and her love of reading, my father, Craig, for his wicked sense of humor which has helped me laugh at even the hardest of situations, and to my brother Zach, who's quickness never fails to keep me down to earth.

The biggest of thanks to Josh, without him pushing me I never would have seized this opportunity. His warmth, love and kindness carry me through every day and healed those wounds I wrote about no so long ago. I love you.

To Abbey, Kate, Emma, Nathanael, Jack, Tyler, and the many other friends and supportive people in my life – thank you for filling my life with laughs, love and companionship. I hope you find peace and success and I thank you for endlessly contributing to mine.

And to you, the reader, whoever you may be: thank you. I hope it brings you whatever you need it to, and thank you for reading it.

To you;

Thank you.

1.

We are not often enough told

The story of our origin,

Though it is one of resounding beauty -

For we are the descendants of stars.

A billion years ago

The blood in our veins

Was the light of the sun,

And the air in our lungs

Was the fallout of asteroids.

And then from these dimensions

We grew

Until we now can see our home.

And though we all must die

Our family,

The stars,

Are waiting quietly for us

To return to them.

- And heavens know I wanna go home

2.

Under the roaring stars,

You smelled like alcohol

And tasted like woodfire smoke

And how could I forget

The bittersweet combination

As your hands wander under my shirt,

My mind buzzed with the static

That your cold fingers burned

Across my stomach in

A bittersweet moment of intimacy

And the line, like my sight, becomes blurrier

As I struggle to stay in it much longer

And that campfire lit night where you touched

Me for the first time and the last has become

A bittersweet memory

And now when I think about it

It leaves a bad taste in my mouth

Because you don't remember how cold that night

Still makes me feel inside, but I still became

More bitter than sweet.

3.

Every word that flowered out of my soul

And onto the page

Was only there because

You rubbed them into me

Through my skin

During those hot nights

When the sheets ended up on the hotel floor

As we tumbled, hungrily

And the feel of your bones

Was ingrained in my fingerprints

I wrote those poems for you

To taste my love on your lips

And to whisper them across

the canyon of the pillows

In the sticky night

And yet somehow, even then I knew,

You would never even read them.

    - Now I have a muse who laughs with me (about you).

4.

I stare my flabby flesh down

With a disgust that burns deep

Within my protruding gut as

I look at my own oily face

In the mirror

Loathing, I reach inside my

Beautiful-scarred-fractured

Mind; tainted with the stretch marks

Of time and the purple-blue bruises

From love and the shallow man-made cuts

Of the hurt that has so shaped me

With that, I forge my new body on the page

Out of words of poems that spill from my mouth

Like the blackened blood of the pen;

The words that distract the world

From my spilling over waist,

My chubby cheeks

And my slightly-lopsided chest

And my furiously scribbled pages

Distract me from the fact

That my mind and body

Are even conjoined at all.

– I made myself in my writing

5.

Once upon a time,

I gave you everything my

Bubblegum heart could muster

And you looked me in the eye +

Spat on it, dissolving my purity

More

And More

And More

Until there was nothing but vinegar left inside me.

And now I wish I could take back

Every sweet thing I ever said to you

And shovel them back into my mouth

Because I deserve to taste that sweetness

More

And I wish I could feel the sugar rush back into my blood

And my teeth could mash faster and faster

To gobble back the innocence, you destroyed

And I wish I could be that candy coated girl

Once more

I could write you

A million sonnets

But they would never

Fully encapsulate

How my heart beats

Only for you

- There aren't enough words in any language, my love

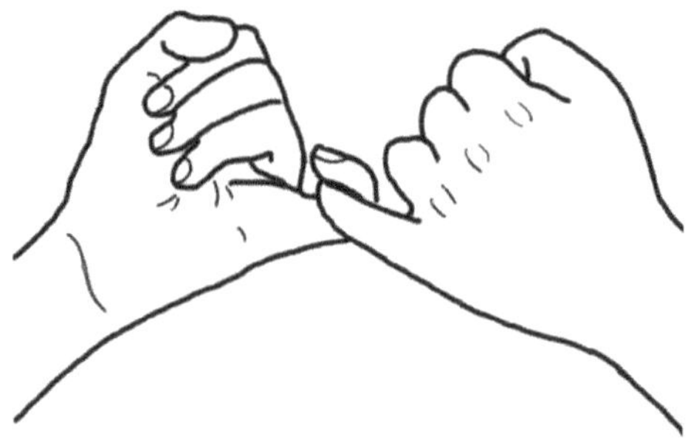

7.

The night is warm and rough as whiskey

And I am intoxicated by its gentle ferocity

As it seeps through my veins, choking

Me as I lay, like plywood, sleepless;

My drunken mind paints a beautiful contradiction

Of youthful joy and an ancient suffering

Encapsulated into a crumbling marble corpse:

I am a spectator to myself breaking.

The prospect of my lives looming,

Drunken laughter echoes

Over the ruins of my sanity and

Of gods like me, long forgotten.

As the liquor-tinged night gives way to day

I push the rubble of my mind back

I may be forgotten by the masses but I am whole

In the broken world I created for myself.

8.

If it's true

That you don't realise how toxic something is

Until it is gone and you are free

Them I wonder if when I'm gone

Will people suddenly feel

l i g h t e r

Without my poison in their blood?

- Thorns of a blackened rose

9.

I have stolen the stars

And torn their atoms from them

To create the essence of myself

And they

Are

Wasted

H e r e

                                        - I am the dark side of stardust

10.

I inhale deep

Pulling with it the familiarity

of your embrace

And I smile, softly,

Maybe the timing was poor

But as your chest falls under my head

Exhale

I feel the light rushing in

It always felt right

In that quiet moment

When we both inhale,

I relish in how natural it feels

To be lost in you

But as the exhale falls,

I remember the aching loneliness

And I quietly question if that comfort is equal to

The progress I abandoned

The pain always seemed worth it

Inhale

Swallow the tears

The disappointment, the grief

And bury it back in my mind

Because you still smile at me with bright eyes and empty words

And while the darkness is encroaching

The corners of my world,

The worst part of it all

Is the exhale doesn't release the crushing pain in my chest

11.

I'd write you a poem, my angel

But heaven already crafted it in your laugh

And planted blooming flowers in my lungs

Whenever you look at me

And those whiskey-laced eyes, my angel

They take away my ability

To put pen to paper and capture

How much I adore you.

- You take the words right out of my mouth

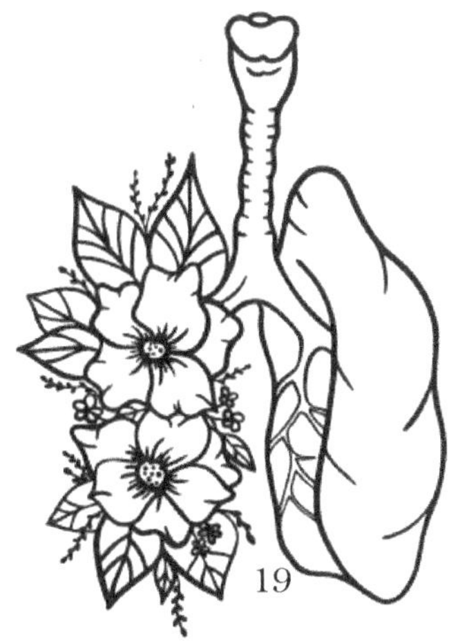

19

12.

I keep hearing a clock tick, lowly,

In the back of my mind

Reminding me softly of how little

Time I have left to do all those

Brilliant things I dreamed

But I am only one person, and

The time seems to slip me by

And I spend more of it worrying

About what I've done than enjoying it

I am still young +

Have so much time left to run

Out on those precious little things

But because the clock will tick regardless

Of how long I stare at the hands

I curse the seconds again.

21

13.

The rise and fall of the chest

Is evidence enough of life

But mine is an empty chasm

Billowing in the wind

And the miracles turn into tragedies

As the days feel longer

And living quickly becomes

That pesky thing between slumbers

Because everything hurts

I wish I knew why

But I have no better explanation

Besides "the tests came back fine"

And living each day at a time

Becomes a painful burden;

I am my own worst enemy -

The echo in my head confirms it

But each day, I billow through

I try to smile but its void in my eyes

Because it's all in the dichotomy

Of being dead while alive

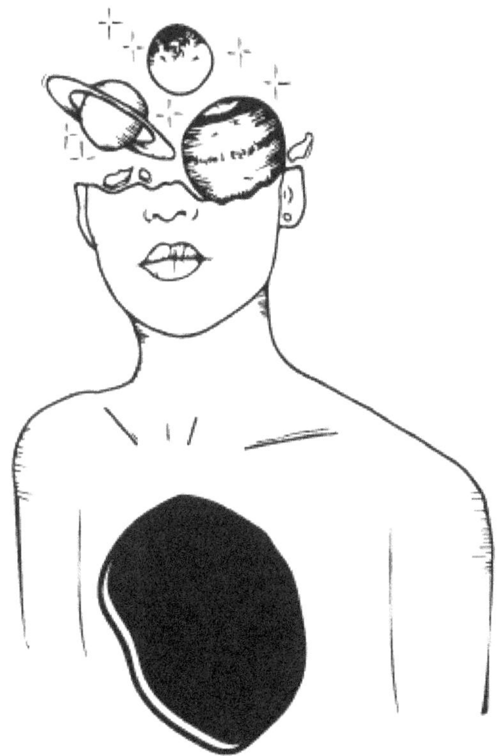

14.

My body is a temple

You worship at my altar

Your hands caress my stomach,

Etching warmth into the crease

Under my breasts

My body is a temple

You worship at my altar

You bite at my flesh

Like a eucharist

And drink my sweet wine

My body is a temple

You worship at my altar

The feeling of your hot

Breath against my shoulder

As you move, quietly, rapidly, with me

My body is a temple

You worship at my altar

The sacrifice is painful

But it quickly fades

As Heaven crashes
down around me

My body is a temple

And you are the deity it
belongs to

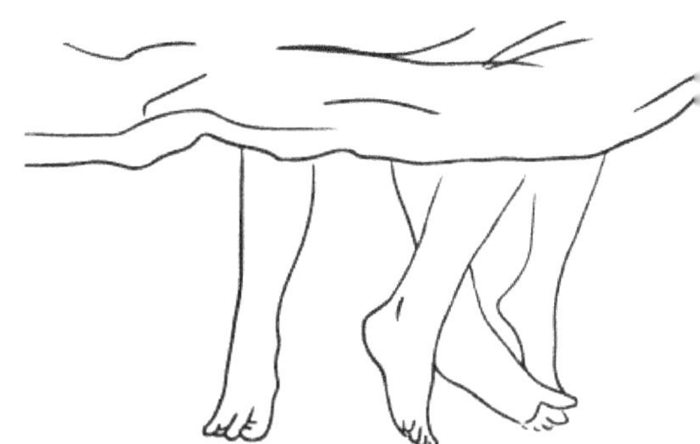

15.

I wish that I could move

The pain that lingers

Behind my eyes + within

My soul out from me

And onto this very page

Alas, I continue to stare at

Sepia tinged nothing, as

The pain eats what's left

Of my chipped fingernails

Against the smudged keyboard

The page is empty as I

Continue to search for something –

Anything to tell you how broken

I feel - it will never come to be,

But goddamnit, I sure will try.

One day

Enough of the sands

Of time will have fallen + buried

The memory of you deep within

One day

Enough of the pain

From your betrayal will have faded

And my scar tissue soul can finally

Begin to heal onwards

One day

You will have not touched me

Or my mind and I will be anew

So I can put you behind me

One day

You won't matter to me anymore

And there will be nothing left for you

To own anymore.

17.

Oh, the way you make me giggle like

A silly six-year-old girl

While dragging me by my ankles

Across your hardwood floor

Oh, the way you hold me tightly in

A single bed against the April night

And your hands warm my virgin skin

Delicately under the covers

Oh, the way you bring butterflies

Into my life with the deep rumble of

Your voice at daybreak after I accidentally

Elbowed you in the face

Oh, the way we walked, hand

In hand through the exhibits

Comparing our beauties to old bones

And sneaking kisses under model stars

Oh, the way you made me spill my guts

That month later when champagne

Blurred my vision and you laughed over

The phone as you spewed them back

Oh, the way you made me fall helplessly

In love with you and oh, my god

The way I can only begin to fall more

And more in love with you each day.

- I'll always be yours, my angel

18.

My bones belong to the sea

Because like the salt

water, they float as driftwood

For the survivors to cling to

My bones belong to the sand

Because like the grains of glass

They are shards glued back together

For the losers to hold as trophies

My bones belong to the wind

Because they race forward

Towards the broken, like the icy

Breeze drying tears on their faces

My bones belong to the flowers

Because like the petals

They are delicate and the brutes'

Rough, callous touches will break them

My bones belong to the dirt

Because like the damp,

Oozing mud, they mould me

Into whoever the critics want me to be

My bones belong to the stars

Because like the supernova

They are dust gathered

In a human void to serve the masses

My bones belong to the earth

And they belong the sky –

In fact, my bones belong

To everyone but me.

– "I am only worth what I provide others."

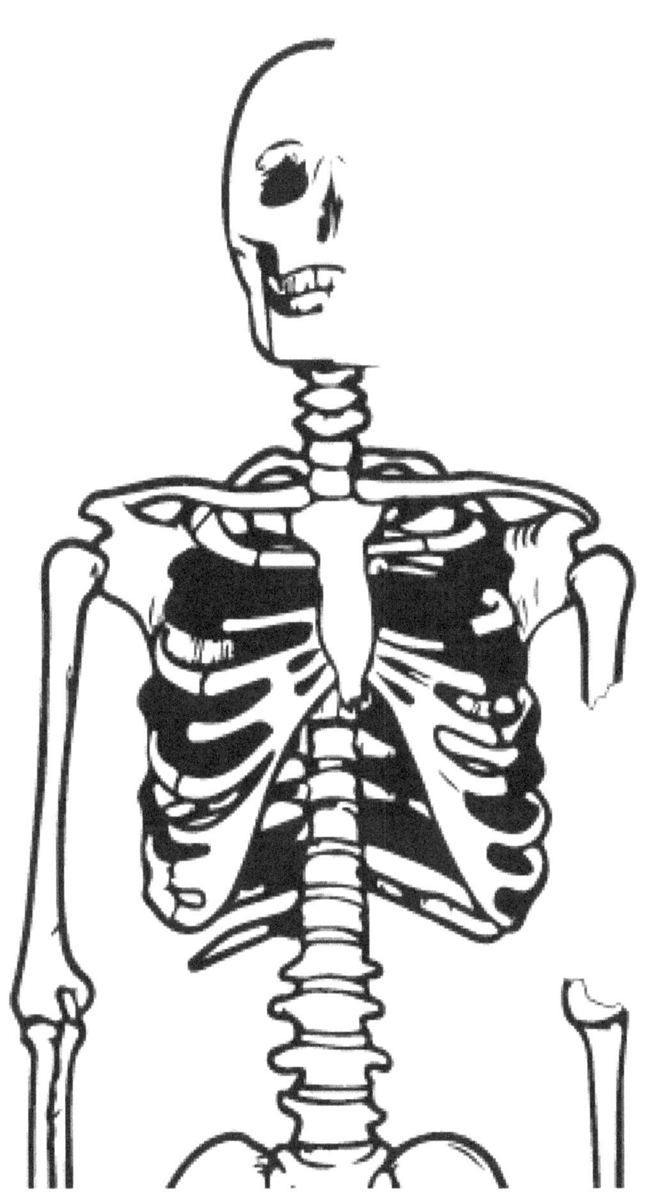

19.

Her name meant something like violets

She was as delicate as the flower, too

A fire deep in her eyes

That warmed my tepid coffee

From across the ravine of the table

She spoke with a lilt that swelled

In my ears like an incoming tide

Of sun-warmed ocean water on

A beach she took me to on a day

Where she wanted me to touch her soul

And she made me fall in love at that table

When her hands painted her words in the air

And her laugh made me understand what

Life was meant to be about and I knew

She was the one made for me

So with every syllable I swam in her

Honey voice and moonbeam smile and

on that cold winter's day, we sat

And she taught me about her beautiful

World and I knew I wanted to live in it

Because I was hers, completely

But she was my soulmate, and hers waltzed

In the door and kissed her hello before

She could even take her eyes off of me

And her smile held something new, unattainable

A peace and gentleness that I could never

Even dream to own because she

Was a wildfire who could only tame herself

And she only holds that restraint for

Him and not the stranger across the table

But at least now I can pretend she's mine

as I clutch onto how we laughed

And loved one another for a millisecond

Across a café table in the freezing cold

Because she had such a beautiful name.

-    And it meant something like violets

20.

I hold out the hope

That this tiny leaflet of pages

Which holds the crevices of my soul,

Will be a well-loved collection to

My home library that my spouse

And I giggle about over coffee

I hope that one day

I can read these poems to my children

As bedtime stories and epics of

The love and loss and triumphs;

Of the life and times of a

Twenty-something trainwreck

And I hope they all will laugh and

Cry with me as they look back on my

Stories and they can doodle in the margins

Of this collection that has sat, collecting

Dust on the coffee table of their living room

Year after year after year

And I hope that one day,

Once all is said done,

Those who I love and lost

Will read these poems too,

And know that they hold my soul

In soft copy in their hands

I know I am a silly little girl,

And I have much yet to do

But these small lines,

They are the me my world remembers

And I hope they can treat her

With as much love as I do

- The future hopes of a young, aimless dreamer.

www.ingramcontent.com/pod-product-compliance
Lightning Source LLC
Chambersburg PA
CBHW060229170726
48004CB00004BA/1487